TO

FROM

DATE

Mothers
Are Heaven's Scent

The Beauty and Fragrance of a Mother's Heart

PAULA J. FOX

Published by Inspired Faith
1952 McDowell Road
Suite 300
Naperville, Illinois 60563
800-900-3427

Design and production: Koechel Peterson & Associates, Inc., Minneapolis, MN

Cover and inside artwork by Katia Andreeva. Artwork designs are reproduced under license from Koechel Peterson & Associates, Minneapolis, MN, and may not be reproduced without permission.

Printed in the United States of America

ISBN 978-1-60810-041-5

02 WOZ 11

Dedication

To these beautiful flowers in my garden...

To my mother, Margaret Argenbright...
  who loved me first and with a forever love...
  my mother, my friend and my most devoted
  fan...what a blessing!

To my grandmother, Ethel Stephenson...
  who always loved me unconditionally...
  what a special treasure!

To my mother-in-love, Grethel Fox...
  who welcomed me into her heart and loved
  me as her own...what a gift!

And to my children...
  Casey, Elena, Darin and Hannah...
  who make me so proud to be a mother myself...
  You are the joy...the *Sunflowers*...of my life!

Table of Contents

beauty.

The Beauty and Fragrance of a Mother's Heart

Mothers are like flowers . . . each one is uniquely beautiful in her own way, and each is designed by God to bloom where she is planted.

The Lord created a variety of different flowers to show us the beauty in His diversity, and He uses them in His written Word to illustrate how we are to be like flowers . . . a reflection of His beauty, spreading His fragrance throughout our world. *"Through us [He] diffuses the fragrance of His knowledge in every place. For we are to God the fragrance of Christ"* (2 Corinthians 2:14–15 NKJV).

This is especially true of Mothers. Not only are they sent from heaven for a very special purpose, but they are also heaven's SCENT, as they are given the awesome responsibility of being the life-giving

aroma of God in their homes. What a beautiful picture! As a Mother is conformed more and more into the image of Christ, she *"reflect[s] like a mirror the glory of the Lord"* (2 Corinthians 3:18 PHILLIPS).

Walk with me now through the Lord's own garden as we look closely at some of His extraordinary creations. The heart of God . . . the beauty and heavenly fragrance of Christ Himself . . . can be seen in each of these flowers and is reflected in a Mother's heart.

Take a good look at God's wonders. They'll take your breath away.

PSALM 66:5 MSG

glory

Baby's Breath

Our first flower reminds us of the very *beginning* of a woman's life as a Mother... the moment when she takes her first child into her arms and smells the fragrance of that sweet *Baby's Breath*. Her heart will never be the same again.

God settles the barren woman in her home as a happy Mother of children.

PSALM 113:9 NIV

[God] created my inmost being;
[He] knit me together in my Mother's womb.
I praise [Him] because I am fearfully
and wonderfully made.

PSALM 139:13–14 NIV

Children are a blessing and a gift from the LORD.

Psalm 127:3 (CEV)

beginnin

Motherhood is a partnership with God.

Red Rose

The *Red Rose* symbolizes a *Mother's* love for her child. When a woman becomes a Mother, she begins to understand more fully the great love God has as a parent for each of us as His children.

How great is the love
the Father has lavished on us,
that we should be called
the children of God!

1 JOHN 3:1 NIV

*L*ove is patient and kind. Love is not jealous or boastful
or proud or rude. Love does not demand its own way. Love is not irritable,
and it keeps no record of when it has been wronged.

1 CORINTHIANS 13:4–5 NLT

Not until I became a Mother did I understand how
much my Mother had sacrificed for me.
Not until I became a Mother did I feel how hurt my
Mother was when I disobeyed.
Not until I became a Mother did I know how proud my
Mother was when I achieved.
Not until I became a Mother did I realize how much
my Mother loves me.

VICTORIA FARNSWORTH

love

Dogwood

The *Dogwood* is a picture of the sacrifice of a Mother's love. The blossoms are formed in the shape of a cross with the crown of thorns in the center and the nail prints at the tip of each petal, reminding us of the ultimate sacrifice of our Lord. A Mother's love enables her to give up her right to personal freedom in order to care for her baby. She is willing to sacrifice "self" for the sake of her child, just as the Lord Jesus sacrificed Himself for each of us.

Live a life of love, just as Christ loved us and gave himself up for us as a fragrant offering and sacrifice to God.

EPHESIANS 5:2 NIV

sacrifice

Before you were conceived, I wanted you.

Before you were born, I loved you.

Before you were here an hour, I would die for you.

This is the **miracle** of life.

MAUREEN HAWKINS

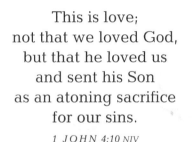

This is love;
not that we loved God,
but that he loved us
and sent his Son
as an atoning sacrifice
for our sins.

1 JOHN 4:10 NIV

The deepest fountains of love are found
at the cross of Christ and in a Mother's heart.

AUTHOR UNKNOWN

Lilac

The *Lilac* represents the *fragrance* of that sacrifice ...the lovely perfumed scent that results when a flower is crushed and gives back to the very one that crushed it. It reminds us of the beauty that surrounds a Mother who "puts on" the gentle character qualities of Christ and wears them like a heavenly perfume...the "fragrance of Christ."

Clothe yourselves with the Lord Jesus Christ. ...with compassion, kindness, humility, gentleness and patience. ...Forgive as the Lord forgave you. And over all these virtues put on love, which binds them all together in perfect unity.

ROMANS 13:14 NIV; COLOSSIANS 3:12–14 NIV

25

*Be kind to each other, tenderhearted, forgiving one another,
just as God through Christ has forgiven you.*

EPHESIANS 4:32 NLT

Everywhere we go, people breathe in the exquisite *fragrance.* Because of Christ, we give off a sweet scent rising to God.

II CORINTHIANS 2:15-16 MSG

fragrance

"Mother" means selfless devotion,
limitless sacrifice and love that
passes understanding.
AUTHOR UNKNOWN

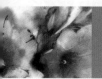

Gladiola

It also takes a lot of *strength* to be a Mother, illustrated by the *Gladiola*…a strong powerful flower that is a favorite in large arrangements because of its size. The name *Gladiola* comes from a Greek word meaning "sword," reminding us of the Bible, which is called "the Sword of the Spirit." This flower represents the Mother who gets her strength from the Lord and the power of His Word. She's prepared to fight for her children in the battle against the evil of this world. God describes this battle in Ephesians 6 where He says…

Be strong in the Lord and the power of His might. …and take …the sword of the Spirit, which is the word of God.

EPHESIANS 6:10, 17 NKJV

*I am convinced
that the influence
of an army
of godly women
will be incalculable—
in our homes,
our churches,
and our culture.*
NANCY LEIGH DEMOSS

A mother's heart is a portrait of *"fighting love"* that will not stop beating for what is best for her children. She is a valiant warrior who will never quit hoping, helping or believing.

JILL RHODES

God says, "Fear not, for I am with you;
be not dismayed, for I am your God.
I will strengthen you, yes, I will help you.
I will uphold you with My righteous right hand."

ISAIAH 41:10 NKJV

strength

Hydrangea

The *Hydrangea* has a wonderful quality of being able to change color from shades of pink to blue, reminding us that a Mother has to be able to adapt to the needs of both girls and boys. Initially, it was thought that this flower was like a chameleon, changing color to match its surroundings. But experiments proved that the color is actually determined by the kind of soil it is planted in. This illustrates the Mother who is planted firmly in the Word of God. She does not allow the world to squeeze her into its mold and determine the color of her thoughts and behavior. Instead, she is transformed by the Lord, through His Word, into the image of Christ.

Be not conformed to this world, but be transformed by the renewing of your mind.

ROMANS 12:2 KJV

$\mathcal{B}$lessed are those who trust in the LORD and have made the LORD their hope and confidence. They are like trees planted along a riverbank, with roots that reach deep into the water. Such trees are not bothered by the heat or worried by long months of drought. Their leaves stay green, and they never stop producing fruit.

JEREMIAH 17:7–8 NLT

My Mother planted seeds of faith and watered them with love.

ALICE GRAY

Mighty oaks from little acorns grow.

Author Unknown

Magnolia

The *Magnolia* blossom grows up high on a huge tree, popular in the South, that spreads its heavenly fragrance for miles. It is among the first of the flowering plants, and fossil magnolias have been found that date back to the time of dinosaurs. They are imprinted with the image of *Magnolia* blossoms that look just like the ones we have today. This flower represents God's unchanging purpose for Mothers since the beginning of time...which was and is to reproduce HIS image in their children for generations to come.

God created man in His own image; in the image of God He created him; male and female He created them. Then God blessed them and said to them, "Be fruitful and multiply..."

GENESIS 1:27–28 NKJV

purpose

A hundred years from now it will not matter
what my bank account was, the sort of house I lived in,
or the kind of car I drove, but the world may be different
because I was important in the life of a child.

Forest E. Witcraft

Train up a child in the way he should go,
and when he is old he will not depart from it.

PROVERBS 22:6 KJV

There is a vast difference between seeing our children just as our children and seeing them as our disciples. If they're just our children, then our only concerns are ... to feed and clothe them, get them into the right schools, well married, etc. But if they're also our disciples, then, more than anyone else, within those twenty or so precious years we have them, we're to teach them everything Jesus has taught us.

Anne Ortlund

Water Lily

This beautiful *Water Lily* was designed by God to be a picture of tranquility as it floats serenely on top of the water. It reminds us of the *serene* beauty of a Mother who brings all her burdens to the Lord in prayer and is able to rest in the water of His Holy Spirit.

Jesus said, "Come unto me all of you that are weary and overburdened, and I will give you rest."

MATTHEW 11:28 NIV

41

No ordinary work done by a man is either as hard or as responsible as the work of a Mother who is bringing up a family of small children. ...for upon her time and strength demands are made not only every hour of the day but often every hour of the night.

Mrs. Theodore Roosevelt

Cast your burden on the Lord, releasing the weight of it, and He will sustain you; He will never allow the righteous to be made to slip, fall, or fail.

PSALM 55:22 AMP

There remains therefore a rest for the [godly Mother].
For [she] who has entered His rest has [herself] also ceased
from [her] works as God did from His. Let us therefore
be diligent to enter that rest.

HEBREWS 4:9–11 NKJV

rest

Bird of Paradise

44

God created the *Bird of Paradise* to actually look like a beautiful bird in flight. Being a Mother can be very exhausting at times, but this flower illustrates the Mother who trusts in the Lord to give her "wings to fly" when she has no more strength of her own.

[She] that waits upon the LORD shall renew [her] strength; [she] shall mount up with wings as an eagle; [she] shall run, and not be weary; and [she] shall walk, and not faint.

ISAIAH 40:31 KJV

$\mathcal{I}$ would get so tired taking care of the children, the house, the wear and tear of Mothering and homemaking. ... This verse was a great comfort to me: *"Now therefore, our God, the great, mighty and awesome God . . . Do not let all this hardship seem trifling in your eyes." (Nehemiah 9:32 NIV)*

Ruth Bell Graham

His strength is perfect when our strength is gone.

He'll carry us when we can't carry on.

Raised in *His power* the weak become strong.

His strength is perfect. His strength is perfect.

STEVEN CURTIS CHAPMAN

wings to fly³

[God] told me, My grace
is enough; it's all you need.
My strength comes into its own
in your weakness. ... Now I take
limitations in stride ... I just let
Christ take over! And so the weaker
I get, the stronger I become.

2 CORINTHIANS 12:9–10 MSG

The name of this gorgeous flower, the *Peony*, comes from the Greek word *paean*, meaning "hymn of praise." What a beautiful picture it gives us of the Mother whose life is like a *"hymn of praise"* to the Lord . . . not only in the way she speaks (her words and the tone of her voice), but also in the way she serves others, she gives glory and honor to the Lord.

If she speaks, she does it as one speaking the very words of God.
If she serves, she does it with the strength God provides, so that in all
things God may be praised through Jesus Christ.

1 PETER 4:11 NIV

*Give unto the LORD the glory
due His name; worship the LORD
in the beauty of holiness.*

PSALM 29:2 KJV

*Whatever you do,
whether in word or deed,
do it all in the name of the Lord
Jesus, giving thanks to God
the Father through Him.*

COLOSSIANS 3:17 NIV

A Mother is a person who, seeing there are only four pieces of pie for five people, promptly announces she never did care for pie.

Tenneva Jordan

hymn of praise

Daylily

The *Daylily* gets its name from the fact that although the plants themselves bloom for weeks, each blossom lasts only one day. We are reminded of the Mother who lives each day to the fullest as if it were her last...as a precious gift from God. She finds joy and creates beauty in the present moment rather than regretting the past or fearing what the future may bring. She says with the Psalmist...

each day

*This is the day
which the LORD has
made. I will rejoice
and be glad in it.*

PSALM 118:24 KJV

53

each day

Jesus said to all the people:
If any of you want to be my followers,
you must forget about yourself. You must take up
your cross each day and follow me.

LUKE 9:23 CEV

Always be joyful and never stop

praying. Whatever happens, keep

thanking God because of Jesus Christ.

This is what God wants you to do.

1 THESSALONIANS 5:16–18 CEV

Blessed is the woman who listens to me,
watching daily at my doors, waiting at my doorway.
For whoever finds me finds life and receives
favor from the LORD.

PROVERBS 8:34–35 NIV

Orchid

The *Orchid* is considered one of the loveliest and most valuable of flowers and symbolizes the Mother who is highly *valued*, not for her external features or material possessions, but for her beautiful Christlike character...the godly wisdom and grace that are beyond measure by the standards of this world.

A woman of noble character who can find?
She is worth far more than rubies.

PROVERBS 31:10 NIV

valued³

She is clothed with strength and dignity; she can laugh at the days to come. She speaks with wisdom, and faithful instruction is on her tongue. She watches over the affairs of her household and does not eat the bread of idleness. Her children arise and call her blessed.

PROVERBS 31:25–28 NIV

A woman who fears the LORD is to be praised.

PROVERBS 31:30 NIV

Mothers are like fine collectibles …
as the years go by they increase in value.

Author Unknown

Sunflower

Sunflowers remind us of joy . . . such bright happy flowers . . . and the secret of their joy is that they always face the sun. This flower represents the Mother who finds her source of joy in the Son of God—the more she seeks His face and turns toward Him, the more her joy overflows into the lives of others.

*The joy of the LORD
is [her] strength.*

NEHEMIAH 8:10 NIV

Taking joy in life is a woman's best cosmetic.

Rosalind Russell

Tucking Ned in bed one night, I leaned down to kiss him good night. Looking closely at my face, a delighted smile spread over his. "It looks just like sunshine," he said. "What looks like sunshine?" I asked. And his fingers gently touched the lines going out from the corners of my eyes. With such an observation, how could anyone mind growing old?

Ruth Bell Graham

[The Mother who looks to the LORD]
for help will be radiant with joy; no shadow
of shame will darken [her] face.

PSALM 34:5 NLT

joy³

Anemones are considered by some to be sacred flowers, thought to possibly be the beautiful "lilies of the field" that Jesus mentioned in the Sermon on the Mount when He said:

> *"Consider the lilies of the field,*
> *how they grow...if God so clothe the grass*
> *of the field, which today is, and tomorrow*
> *is cast into the oven, shall he not*
> *much more clothe you...?"*

MATTHEW 6:28, 30 KJV

Legend also tells us that this flower got its gorgeous deep color from the royal blood of Jesus that dropped on it when it was growing at the foot of the cross. This illustrates the Mother whose beauty comes from being clothed in the *beauty* and righteousness of Christ.

clothed

Clothe yourselves with the
Lord Jesus Christ, and do not think
about how to gratify the desires
of the sinful nature.

ROMANS 13:14 NIV

❧

But you are the ones chosen by God,
chosen for the high calling of priestly work,
chosen to be a holy people, God's instruments
to do his work and speak out for him, to tell
others of the night-and-day difference he made
for you—from nothing to something,
from rejected to accepted.

1 PETER 2:9 MSG

ost of all the other beautiful things in life come in twos and
threes, by dozens and hundreds. Plenty of roses, stars, sunsets,
rainbows, brothers and sisters, aunts and cousins, but only one
Mother in the whole wide world.

Kate Douglas Wiggin

Azalea

A blooming *Azalea* bush can range in color from bright red to fuchsia and is often described with terms such as "fiery" and "flaming" as in reference to a "burning bush." It gives us a picture of the Mother who is on fire with a passion for the Lord. She is filled with His Holy Spirit to such an extent that she gives off sparks that ignite and inspire others as well. In Scripture, God is often revealed as a fire, and the Bible tells us the Lord will...

"...baptize you with the Holy Spirit and with fire."

MATTHEW 3:11 NIV

Never lag in zeal and in earnest
endeavor; be aglow and burning with
the Spirit, serving the Lord.

ROMANS 12:11 AMP

Fan into flame the gift of God,
which is in you ... For God did not give us
a spirit of timidity, but a spirit of power,
of love and of self-discipline.

2 TIMOTHY 1:6–7 NIV

Mother love is the fuel

that *enables* a normal human

being to do the impossible.

MARION GARRETTY

fire

Queen Anne's Lace

Queen Anne's Lace is a delicate, lacy flower often used in weddings. It symbolizes the Mother who has developed an intimate relationship with Jesus and has entered into a special union with Him (like marriage), where she has committed her life to Him. The Bible calls her the "bride of Christ," and she knows deep within her soul that she can trust Him completely because He loves her and will always delight in her.

As a bridegroom rejoices over his bride,
so will your God rejoice over you.

ISAIAH 62:5 NIV

bride of Christ

Know that the LORD has set apart
for Himself [the woman] who is godly; the LORD
will hear when [she] calls to Him.

PSALM 4:3 NKJV

You will show me the path of life; in Your
presence is fullness of joy; at Your right hand
are pleasures forevermore.

PSALM 16:11 NKJV

Love the LORD your God with all your heart, all your soul,
and all your strength. Always remember these commands I
give you today. Teach them to your children, and talk about
them when you sit at home and walk along the road, when
you lie down and when you get up.

DEUTERONOMY 6:5–7 NCV

Forsythia

A *Forsythia* bush asserts itself every spring with brilliant blasts of yellow blossoms. It stands out as a bold and showy plant that God uses to display this powerful aspect of His character. It represents the Mother who has boldness and courage to face the challenges of her life. She is not afraid because she knows that the Lord is always right there with her and will enable her with His strength, His power and His courage.

"Be strong and courageous!
Do not be afraid or discouraged.
For the LORD your God is with
you wherever you go."

JOSHUA 1:9 NLT

[She] does not fear bad news,
nor live in dread of what may happen.
For [she] is settled in [her] mind that Jehovah
will take care of [her]. This is why [she] is
not afraid but can calmly face [her] foes.

PSALM 112:7–8 TLB

❧

Have no fear of sudden disaster
or of the ruin that overtakes the wicked,
for the LORD will be your confidence and
will keep your foot from being snared.

PROVERBS 3:25–26 NIV

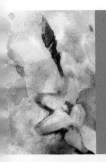

No language can express the power and beauty and heroism and majesty of a Mother's love. It shrinks not where man cowers, and grows stronger where man faints.

E. H. Chapin

Daisy

The *Daisy* is a happy little flower that got its name, *day's eye*, from the Anglo-Saxons, because the original little English daisy closes at nightfall and opens again at sunrise. This illustrates the day-to-day life of the Mother who walks with the Lord. She has no part in the darkness of this world, but lives in the light of Christ.

Jesus ... said, "I am the light of the world.
Whoever follows me will never walk in darkness,
but will have the light of life."

JOHN 8:12 NIV

81

If we are living in the light
of God's presence, just as Christ does,
then we have wonderful fellowship
and joy with each other.

1 JOHN 1:7 TLB

The process of shaping the child … shapes also the Mother herself. Reverence for her sacred burden calls her to all that is pure and good, that she may teach primarily by her own humble daily example.

Elisabeth Elliot

The bright light of Christ makes your way plain.
So no more stumbling around. Get on with it! The good, the right,
the true—these are the actions appropriate for daylight hours.
Figure out what will please Christ, and then do it.

EPHESIANS 5:8 MSG

light

Delphinium

The name *Delphinium* comes from the Greek word for *dolphin*, because it is shaped like the nose of the bottlenose dolphin. This beautiful creature moves with such grace in the water, reminding us of the grace of a Mother's love when she abides in the living water of the Holy Spirit. This grace is not the physical kind, but rather a Christlike quality. This grace means treating others with kindness and love even when they least deserve it . . . as a gift . . . like God's love for us.

For by grace are you saved through faith, and that not of yourselves; it is a gift of God, not of works, lest any man should boast.

EPHESIANS 2:8–9 KJV

She opens her mouth
with wisdom and on her tongue
is the law of kindness.

PROVERBS 31:26 NKJV

❧

"Parenting by heart" . . .
is giving our children the grace to fail
and the strength to get back up again simply
by opening our hearts to lead the way.

HELEN BURNS

The reason that some Mothers get along better

in this life is because they have learned to be

kinder than necessary to all who need it.

AUTHOR UNKNOWN

grace

The *Calla Lily* gets its name from the Greek word *kalos*, which means "beautiful." It illustrates the beauty of a Mother's love that wraps itself like a protective covering around her children. The white part is actually the bract of the flower, which is usually the green leaf-like underpinning that holds the blossom ... and in this case, it shelters the flowers inside, just as the Lord promises He will do for His children.

[You] spread Your protection over them ...
for surely ... you surround them with
your favor as with a shield.

PSALM 5:11–12 NIV

> She never quite leaves her children at home,
> even when she doesn't take them along.
>
> MARGARET CULKIN BANNING

*Those who respect
the Lord will have security, and their
children will be protected.*

PROVERBS 14:26 NCV

*He orders His angels to protect you
wherever you go. They will steady you with
their hands to keep you from stumbling
against the rocks on the trail.*

PSALM 91:11–12 TLB

protective

Lupine

This beautiful little purple flower called *Lupine* grows wild in the Arizona deserts, thriving in the poorest of soil. It is a picture of the Mother who has learned to be content in all circumstances, displaying amazing beauty and grace regardless of the situation, because she knows that God is her source of living water. The Bible describes her this way:

[She] has learned to be content whatever the circumstances may be. [She] is ready for anything through the strength of the One who lives within [her].

PHILIPPIANS 4:11, 13 PHILLIPS

God will strengthen you
with his own great power so that
you will not give up when troubles come,
but you will be patient.

COLOSSIANS 1:11 NCV

We do not give up. Our physical body is becoming older and weaker, but our spirit inside us is made new every day. We have small troubles for a while now, but they are helping us gain an eternal glory that is much greater than the troubles.

2 CORINTHIANS 4:16–17 NCV

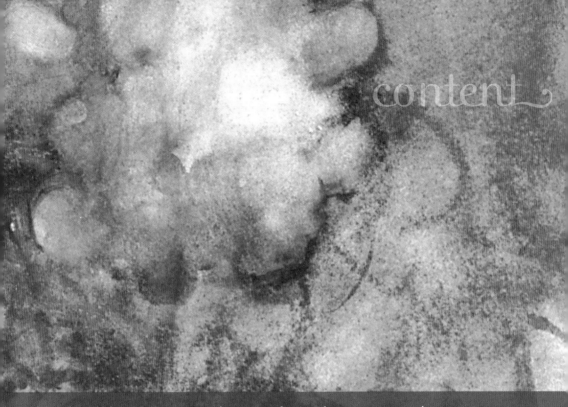

content

A positive mom doesn't take away her children's troubles; she teaches them how to look for the hand of God in the midst of them.

KAROL LADD

Zinnia

The early nickname for the *Zinnia* was "youth and old age," because old flowers stayed fresh even as new flowers on the same stalk began to bloom. It is a reminder that a Mother's physical features may change through the years, but her inner beauty that comes from the Lord does not fade. It becomes even more beautiful with time.

Your beauty should not come from outward adornment...
Instead, it should be that of your inner self, the unfading beauty of a
gentle and quiet spirit, which is of great worth in God's sight.

1 PETER 3:3–4 NIV

The godly shall flourish ... For they
are transplanted into the Lord's own garden and are under
His personal care. Even in old age they will still
produce fruit and be vital and green.

PSALM 92:12–14 TLB

"Even to your old age and gray hairs, I am He, I am

He who will sustain you. I have made you and I will

carry you; I will sustain you and I will rescue you."

ISAIAH 46:4 NIV

Some people, no matter
how old they get, never lose
their beauty...they merely
move it from their faces
into their hearts.

MARTIN BUXBAUM

inner beauty³

Iris

A beautiful purple *Iris* reminds us that the Mother who belongs to the Lord has royal blood in her veins. She is a daughter of the King and goes straight to the throne of God to petition for her family and those she loves. The Iris represents the *prayers* of a godly Mother. The three center petals pointing to heaven symbolize the Lord Himself (Father, Son, and Holy Spirit) living within her heart and making intercession for her in heaven. The outside three petals illustrate the Mother's body, soul, and spirit, bowed humbly before the Lord in prayer. And the Lord promises...

The prayer of a righteous woman is powerful and effective.

JAMES 5:16 NIV

I remember my Mother's prayers
and they have always followed me.
They have clung to me all my life.
All that I am, or hope to be,
I owe to my angel Mother.

Abraham Lincoln

In David's prayer for his son, Solomon, he said, *"Prayer also shall be made for him continually; and daily shall he be praised" (Psalm 72:15 KJV)*. . . . Wouldn't it be wonderful if Mothers and fathers took this suggestion to heart . . . to pray continually and praise daily?

Ruth Bell Graham

"When you first started praying, an answer was given, and I came to tell you, because God loves you very much."

DANIEL 9:23 NCV

prayers

Sweet Peas have little curling tendrils that love to hug things and never let go, reminding us that a Mother's love is very nurturing (lots of hugs) ... and like God's love, it never lets go. It is forever.

[Jesus said,] "I will never leave you nor forsake you."

HEBREWS 13:5 NKJV

forever

Those who know your name
will trust in you, for you, LORD, have never
forsaken those who seek you.

PSALM 9:10 NIV

A Mother holds her children's hands
for a while, but their hearts forever.

AUTHOR UNKNOWN

A father may turn his back on his child; brothers and sisters may become inveterate enemies; husbands may desert their wives and wives their husbands. But a Mother's love endures through all; in good repute, in bad repute, in the face of the world's condemnation a Mother still loves on.

Washington Irving

Daffodil

The *Daffodil* is one of the first bulbs to burst through the cold winter ground, sometimes through the snow itself...and like a beautiful little trumpet, it heralds the coming of spring. It represents fresh hope and is a picture of the Mother who is able to live confidently through the bleak and difficult winter seasons of her life, because her hope is in the Lord and in the promises of His Word.

"For I know the plans I have for you,"
declares the LORD, "plans to prosper you and not to harm you,
plans to give you hope and a future."

JEREMIAH 29:11 NIV

Every mother at some time prays
for a prodigal, knowing there is nothing
more she can do but leave her heart and
home open to the hope of the Lord.

AUTHOR UNKNOWN

hope

O Lord, you alone are my hope:
I've trusted you from childhood. Yes, you
have been with me from birth and have
helped me constantly—no wonder
I am always praising you!

PSALM 71:5–6 TLB

As a Mom, you serve the Most High God, and His dream for your life and your family is so much bigger and better than you can even imagine.

Joel Osteen

Cornflower

The *Cornflower* is a very small flower, but God gave it a special brilliant blue color. In Scripture blue symbolizes heaven, and this little flower reminds us that every Mother, no matter how small and insignificant she may feel, can have a "mountain moving" faith. She can be transformed into the image of God and reflect the *beauty of heaven* and the glory of the Lord in her home.

"Those who are wise will shine like the brightness of the heavens."

DANIEL 12:3 NIV

heaven

"If you have faith as small as a mustard seed,
you can say to this mountain, 'Move from here to there'
and it will move. Nothing will be impossible for you."

MATTHEW 17:20 NIV

The most glorious sight that one ever sees beneath
the stars is the sight of worthy Motherhood.

GEORGE W. TRUETT

The Mother who creates and sustains a home
and under whose hands children grow up to be
strong and pure men and women, is a creator
second only to God.

Helen Hunt Jackson

Gerbera Daisy

A single stem *Gerbera Daisy* looks beautiful all by itself in a vase and represents the Mother who has the faith to *stand alone* for what she believes in. She is not swayed by the pressures of the world around her because she is firmly grounded in God's Word and fully equipped with His spiritual protection to stand her ground.

Put on the full armor of God, so that when the day of evil comes, you may be able to stand your ground.

EPHESIANS 6:13 NIV

"I, the LORD your God, will hold
your right hand, saying unto you,
'Fear not. I will help you.'"

ISAIAH 41:13 NKJV

❧

It is God who arms me with strength
and makes my way perfect. He makes my
feet like the feet of a deer; he enables
me to stand on the heights.

PSALM 18:32–33 NIV

Always be prepared to give an answer to everyone

who asks you to give the *reason* for the hope that

you have. But do this with gentleness and respect.

1 PETER 3:15 NIV

grounded

Chrysanthemum

The name *Chrysanthemum* comes from two Greek words *chrysos* (gold) and *anthos* (flower)—"*gold flower*"—reminding us of the purity and strength of a Mother's love. It is like fine gold...priceless and able to stand the test of time, just as God's love for His children.

How priceless is your unfailing love!

PSALM 36:7 NIV

I love everyone who loves me, and I will be found
by all who honestly search. What you receive from me is more
valuable than even the finest gold or the purest silver.

PROVERBS 8:17, 19 CEV

The little things that make life sweet
are worth their weight in gold;
They can't be bought at any price
and neither are they sold.

ESTELLE WAITE HOOVER

A Mother's love, over the wastes of
worldly fortune, sends the radiance of its
quenchless fidelity like a star in heaven.

E. H. Chapin

gold

Aster

The *Aster* is sometimes called "star flower" because the name comes from the Greek word for *star*. This flower reminds us that a Mother who walks with the Lord is like a bright star that helps to guide her children (and others in her world) to a knowledge of God...just as a star led the three wise men to find the Christ child.

You shine like stars in the universe as you hold out the Word of Life.

PHILIPPIANS 2:15–16 NIV

Direct your children onto the right path, and when they are older, they will not leave it.

PROVERBS 22:6 NLT

For the Mother is and must be, whether she knows it or not, the greatest, strongest, and most lasting teacher her children have.

HANNAH WHITALL SMITH

star

If your children enter adulthood

with a clear concept of who God is

and what He wants them to do,

you will have achieved the

greatest accomplishments in life.

DR. JAMES DOBSON

Easter Lily

The *Easter Lily* symbolizes the resurrection of our Lord. The bulbs appear to be dead when they are planted in the ground, giving us a picture of Christ's death and burial for our sins. On the third day, He rose from the dead in all His glory just like this beautiful flower. It illustrates how *every* Mother can be "born again" to a fresh new life by trusting in the Son of God who loved us and gave His life for us. God wants for us to live with Him for eternity and He promises us abundant life here on earth as well.

"For God so loved the world that He gave His only begotten Son, that whoever believes in Him should not perish but have everlasting life."

JOHN 3:16 NKJV

*A*rise [from the depression and prostration in which circumstances have kept you—rise to a new life]! Shine (be radiant with the glory of the Lord), for your light has come, and the glory of the Lord has risen upon you!

ISAIAH 60:1 AMP

Therefore, if anyone is in Christ, [she] is a new creation; the old is gone, the new has come!

2 CORINTHIANS 5:17 NIV

new life

[Jesus said,] "I have come that they may have life, and that they may have it more abundantly."

JOHN 10:10 NKJV

Carnation

The name *Carnation* comes from the word *incarnation*, referring to the incarnation of God Himself, being made in human form. This flower represents the Mother who has accepted the Lord Jesus Christ as her personal Savior and has invited Him into her life to be her Lord. *God Himself has been incarnated in her heart,* and she carries the "fragrance of Christ" to her world.

> *[She herself] no longer live[s],*
> *but Christ lives in [her]. And the real life [she]*
> *now [has] within [her] body is a result of trusting*
> *in the Son of God, who loved [her] and*
> *gave himself for [her].*

GALATIANS 2:20 TLB

An interesting note on carnations: Although they are one of the most common and least expensive of the cut flowers, their fragrance is one of the sweetest and lasts even after the flower has died...reminding us once again that...

"She herself no longer lives, but Christ lives in her."

We know how much God loves us,
and we have put our trust in his love.
God is love, and all who live in love
live in God and God lives in them.

1 JOHN 4:16 NLT

fragrance of Christ

$\mathcal{Y}$ou will find as you look back upon your life that the moments when you have really lived, are the moments when you have done things in a spirit of love.

Henry Drummond

Live a life of love, just as Christ loved us and gave himself up for us as a fragrant offering and sacrifice to God.

EPHESIANS 5:2 NIV

God wants to transform every Mother
into *HIS image* . . .
to reflect *HIS beauty* . . .
and to carry *HIS fragrance*
to her world.

Now thanks be to God who always leads us in triumph in Christ, and through us diffuses the fragrance of His knowledge in every place. For we are to God the fragrance of Christ...

2 CORINTHIANS 2:14–15 NKJV

Mothers Are Heaven's Scent

Each mother God created has her own unique design
just suited for His purpose, time and place
Like a flower sent from heaven with a *beauty* all her own
and a fragrance that reflects His love and grace

She depends upon the Lord, the Master Gardener in her life
who cares for her, *providing* every need
He knows what kind of soil is best and how she should be pruned
for He planted her from just a tiny seed

God desired to fill the earth with great diversity and style . . .
such differences in color, shape and size
Every mother is *original* . . . no two are quite the same
But every one is special in His eyes

She's designed by God to add a touch of beauty to her world
when she chooses to be a part of His bouquet . . .
With the *fragrance* of the Lord placed within her heart and home
She grows along His path to show the way

As a flower that is crushed gives back the sweetest smell of all
to the very foot that stepped on it, you see . . .
So a mother's love reflects the very love of God's own Son
when she *sacrifices* self for family

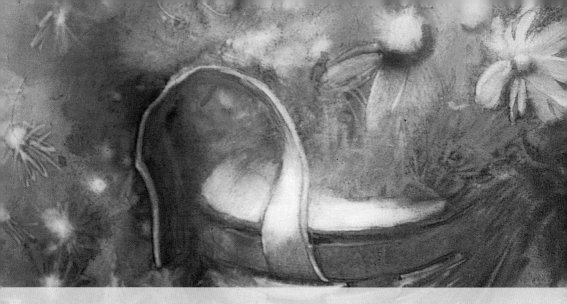

Every right to personal freedom she most willingly gives up

the moment her first child is born . . . and then

The fragrance of her beauty becomes like Heaven's scent . . .

humility that's modeled after Him

And the children that she nurtures in the knowledge of the Lord

are the seeds that become flowers on their own

blooming everywhere God plants them . . . adding beauty to their world

reproducing all the *grace* that they've been shown.

About the Author

Paula J. Fox describes herself as a lifetime student whose passion is to continue learning and applying Godly wisdom in her life so that she can share it with others. Her desire is to inspire and motivate others to live a life of purpose and significance. She is a teacher at heart with a degree in special education and 35 years experience teaching and leading all ages from preschool through adult.

She and her husband, Larry, have three grown children and she is now able to devote more of her time to writing. Besides being a teacher and leader in her own church, she is founder and leader of L'dor (Ladies' day of renewal), a home-based Bible study for women, which has been active now for 25 years. Paula loves researching and writing her own Bible study lessons as well as writing poetry and prose. She also enjoys speaking to women's groups and retreats.

Paula Fox can be contacted at paulajfox@live.com

Encouragement for the Soul

To share how this book has encouraged you
or someone close to you, send us an email at:
feedback@inspiredfaith.com

To read more heartfelt stories,
view life-inspiring movies, enjoy daily devotionals,
quotes and Scriptures to strengthen and inspire
your faith—and to share with a friend—
visit us at www.inspiredfaith.com